Nature's Changes

Animal Life Cycles
Growing and Changing

Bobbie Kalman

Crabtree Publishing Company

www.crabtreebooks.com

Created by Bobbie Kalman

For my cousin Alex Brissenden
Alex, you inspire me! You are intelligent, wise, and such an old soul. You touch my heart.

Author and Editor-in-Chief
Bobbie Kalman

Project editor
Kelley MacAulay

Editors
Molly Aloian
Robin Johnson
Kathryn Smithyman

Design
Katherine Berti
Margaret Amy Salter (back cover)

Production coordinator
Heather Fitzpatrick

Photo research
Crystal Sikkens

Illustrations
Barbara Bedell: back cover, pages 5 (raccoon, earthworm, grasshopper,
    humpback whale, Komodo dragon, ladybug, and monk seal),
    6 (egg and Komodo dragon), 9, 11 (top right and bottom left), 14,
    15 (monk seals), 19, 20, 21, 22 (white and green fish), 26, 27,
    29 (tiny earthworms), 31 (ladybug and raccoon)
Katherine Berti: pages 5 (rattlesnake and sea horse), 6 (snakes),
    15 (rocks), 18, 22 (blue and yellow fish), 23
Bonna Rouse: pages 5 (oriole and frog), 6 (lion), 7 (eggs and baby hatching),
    11 (top left), 16 (bird), 17, 22 (baby salmon), 24, 25, 31 (eggs)
Margaret Amy Salter: pages 5 (koala and spider), 6 (wolf), 7 (embryo), 10,
    11 (bottom right), 28, 29 (all except tiny earthworms), 31 (spider)
Tiffany Wybouw: pages 7 (hatchlings), 12, 16 (eggs), 31 (turtle)

Photographs and reproductions
Robert Thomas: page 13 (art reproduction)
Tom McHugh/Photo Researchers, Inc.: page 10
robertmccaw.com: page 28
Minden Pictures: Mitsuaki Iwago: page 14
© A & A Ferrari/SeaPics.com: page 22
Visuals Unlimited: Jim Merli: page 18
Other images by Corel, Creatas, Digital Stock, Photodisc, and TongRo Image Stock

Crabtree Publishing Company

www.crabtreebooks.com   1-800-387-7650

Copyright © **2006 CRABTREE PUBLISHING COMPANY.**
All rights reserved. No part of this publication may be reproduced,
stored in a retrieval system or be transmitted in any form or by any
means, electronic, mechanical, photocopying, recording, or otherwise,
without the prior written permission of Crabtree Publishing Company.
In Canada: We acknowledge the financial support of the Government
of Canada through the Canada Book Fund for our publishing activities.

Printed in Canada/042013/MA20130325

Cataloging-in-Publication Data
Kalman, Bobbie.
  Animal life cycles : growing and changing / Bobbie Kalman.
      p. cm. -- (Nature's changes)
  Includes index.
  ISBN-13: 978-0-7787-2278-6 (rlb)
  ISBN-10: 0-7787-2278-3 (rlb)
  ISBN-13: 978-0-7787-2312-7 (pbk)
  ISBN-10: 0-7787-2312-7 (pbk)
1. Animal life cycles--Juvenile literature. I. Title. II. Series.
  QL49.K292 2006
  571.8'1--dc22   2005035793
                                                   LC

Published in Canada
Crabtree Publishing
616 Welland Ave.
St. Catharines, Ontario
L2M 5V6

Published in the United States
Crabtree Publishing
PMB 59051
350 Fifth Avenue, 59th Floor
New York, New York 10118

Published in the United Kingdom
Crabtree Publishing
Maritime House
Basin Road North, Hove
BN41 1WR

Published in Australia
Crabtree Publishing
3 Charles Street
Coburg North
VIC 3058

Contents

Animal life cycles

Animals are living things. Living things breathe, eat, grow, and change. There are many kinds of animals. Some are tiny, and others are huge! As animals grow, they go through many **stages**, or sets of changes. The stages that animals go through make up their **life cycles**. Different animals have different life cycles.

Changing animals

Animals are born or hatch from eggs. The animals then grow and change into adults. Adult animals are fully grown and can make babies of their own.

These egret chicks are small next to their tall mother. The babies will grow and change until they are fully grown.

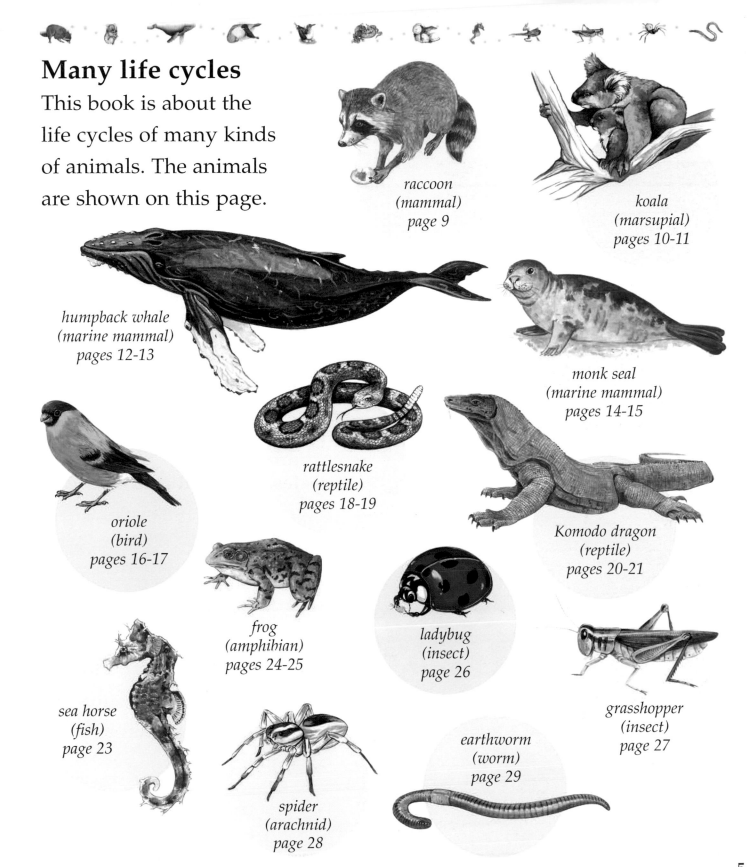

Many life cycles

This book is about the life cycles of many kinds of animals. The animals are shown on this page.

raccoon
(mammal)
page 9

koala
(marsupial)
pages 10-11

humpback whale
(marine mammal)
pages 12-13

monk seal
(marine mammal)
pages 14-15

rattlesnake
(reptile)
pages 18-19

Komodo dragon
(reptile)
pages 20-21

oriole
(bird)
pages 16-17

frog
(amphibian)
pages 24-25

ladybug
(insect)
page 26

grasshopper
(insect)
page 27

sea horse
(fish)
page 23

spider
(arachnid)
page 28

earthworm
(worm)
page 29

Growing embryos

When animals begin to grow, they are called **embryos**. Some embryos grow inside the bodies of their mothers. Other embryos grow inside eggs that are laid by their mothers.

Some animals are born

Animal mothers that have embryos growing inside their bodies are **pregnant**. When an embryo has finished growing, it is **born**. It leaves its mother's body.

*This cheetah mother was pregnant for three months. Then her **cubs**, or baby cheetahs, were born.*

Breaking out

Embryos that do not grow inside the bodies of their mothers grow inside eggs that were laid by their mothers. When the embryos have grown enough, they **hatch**. To hatch is to break out of an egg. Babies that hatch from eggs are called **hatchlings**.

Growing up

Young animals grow and change until they become adults. When they are adults, they are able to **mate**. To mate is to join together to make babies.

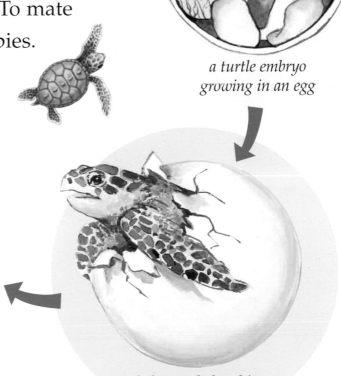

turtle eggs

a turtle embryo growing in an egg

a turtle hatchling

a baby turtle hatching from an egg

Mammals are born

Most **mammal** babies grow and develop inside the bodies of their mothers. Once the babies are born, mammal mothers take care of them. Mammal mothers make milk inside their bodies. The babies drink the milk. Drinking mother's milk is called **nursing**. Nursing gives babies the food they need to grow and develop.

Cows are mammals. This baby cow is nursing.

A raccoon's life cycle

Raccoons are mammals. Mother raccoons have several babies at the same time. A group of babies is called a **litter**. A baby raccoon is called a **kit**. When kits are between two and four months old, they stop nursing and learn how to find food on their own.

Kits live with their mothers for about a year.

*Kits are born in **dens**, or safe shelters. Many raccoon dens are found in trees.*

Adult raccoons can mate and have babies.

*One-year-old raccoons are called **yearlings**. They are playful! They are almost fully grown.*

Joeys in pouches

Koalas are mammals called **marsupials**. Most marsupial mothers have **pouches**, or pockets on the front of their bodies. A koala mother has a pouch that opens near her back legs. A koala embryo grows inside its mother's body for only a short time. When it is very small, the embryo crawls out of its mother's body and into her pouch. The **joey**, or baby koala, nurses and continues to grow inside its mother's pouch.

A koala mother takes good care of her joey.

A koala's life cycle

nursing
joey

When a joey is born, it is about the size of a bean. It cannot see or hear, but it can smell its mother's milk. It crawls across its mother's body to find her pouch. Once it has reached the pouch, the joey begins nursing.

A joey does not leave the pouch until it is about six months old. A six-month-old joey crawls in and out of its mother's pouch. It keeps nursing when it is inside the pouch.

The joey lives with its mother for two to three years. When the joey is three years old, it is an adult. It can mate and have babies of its own.

A one-year-old joey is ready to stop nursing. It begins to climb trees and eat **eucalyptus** leaves. Eucalyptus leaves are the only food that koalas eat.

11

A whale of a journey!

Humpback whales are huge **marine mammals**. Marine mammals live in oceans. Humpback whales **migrate** from cold ocean waters to warm ocean waters. To migrate means to move to a new place for a certain period of time. The whales migrate so that mother whales can have their **calves**, or babies, in warm waters. The calves need to live in warm waters in order to grow. When the calves are big enough, they swim back to the cold ocean waters that will be their summer homes.

A calf's first breath

A whale calf grows inside its mother's body for about a year. Then it is born. As soon as the calf is born, it must swim quickly to the surface of the ocean to take its first breath of air. Like all mammals, whales breathe air using body parts called **lungs**. A newborn calf is not strong enough to swim to the ocean's surface, so its mother gives it a boost.

A mother humpback guides her calf to the water's surface so it can take its first breath of air. Humpback calves are born white.

Putting on the blubber

Humpback whale calves spend about five months in warm ocean waters. The calves grow quickly. Their bodies change to get ready for the cold waters in which they will soon live. Calves cannot survive in cold waters without **blubber**. Blubber is a thick layer of fat. Calves put on blubber by nursing. They nurse a lot! Whale milk is very fatty, so calves put on blubber quickly.

Moving to the cold

When the calves have thick blubber, they are ready for their first long journey to the cold ocean waters. They continue to nurse during the journey. After they arrive in the cold waters, they stop nursing, however. The calves are now **juveniles**. Juveniles leave their mothers to find their own food. Humpback whales become adults when they are between four and eight years old.

*A male humpback often swims with a mother whale and her calf. The male whale is called an **escort**.*

13

Born on land

Like whales, monk seals are marine mammals. Monk seals live mainly in oceans, but their babies are born on land. Monk seal babies are called **pups**. Monk seals are **endangered** animals. There are very few monk seals left on Earth!

A monk seal's life cycle

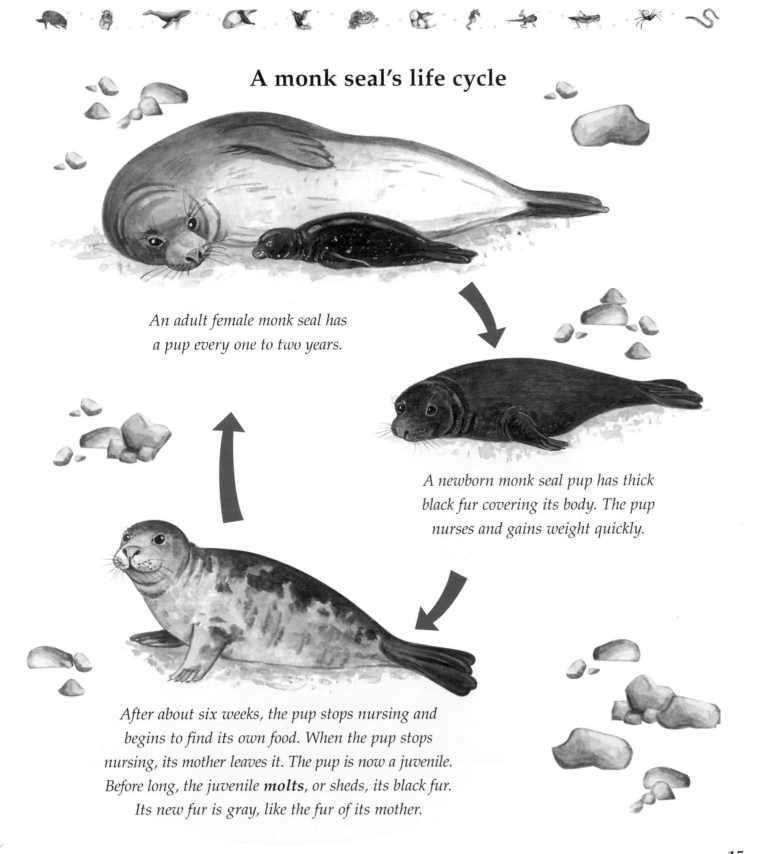

An adult female monk seal has a pup every one to two years.

A newborn monk seal pup has thick black fur covering its body. The pup nurses and gains weight quickly.

*After about six weeks, the pup stops nursing and begins to find its own food. When the pup stops nursing, its mother leaves it. The pup is now a juvenile. Before long, the juvenile **molts**, or sheds, its black fur. Its new fur is gray, like the fur of its mother.*

Birds lay eggs

Many **birds** mate in spring. Soon after mating, female birds lay eggs. Adult birds sit on their eggs to keep the embryos inside them warm.

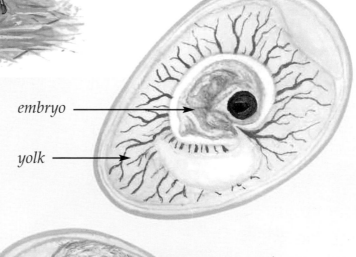

embryo

yolk

Inside an egg

A bird embryo grows inside an egg. There is a **yolk** in the egg with the embryo. The embryo eats the yolk and grows quickly. As it gets bigger, the embryo grows an **egg tooth**. An egg tooth is a sharp part on the embryo's beak. When the embryo is ready to hatch, it uses its egg tooth to crack open the hard shell of the egg.

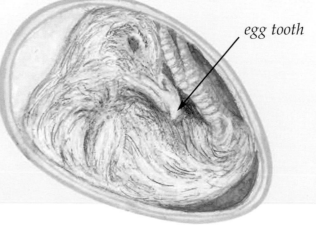

egg tooth

16

Let me out!

When the embryo has grown enough, it hatches from its egg. A baby bird that has just hatched is called a hatchling. The hatchling opens its mouth wide to tell its parents that it wants to be fed. Its parents bring it food. The hatchling grows quickly. Soon it will be an adult that can make babies of its own. Female birds then lay eggs.

oriole egg

CRACK!

oriole hatchling

young oriole

adult oriole

17

Snakes are reptiles

This mother corn snake has laid a clutch of eggs.

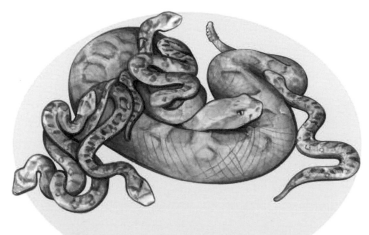

These rattlesnake babies were just born.

Snakes are **reptiles**. Reptiles start their lives inside eggs, just as birds do. Most snake mothers lay groups of eggs called **clutches**. Snakes lay their clutches in cool, damp places. They lay eggs under logs or rocks, in caves, or among leaves. Snake mothers do not care for their eggs. After hatching, the baby snakes find their own food.

Some snakes are born

Some snake mothers do not lay eggs. They carry their eggs inside their bodies. The baby snakes hatch inside the bodies of their mothers. Soon after hatching, the baby snakes are born. Once they are born, the baby snakes leave their mothers. They find their own food.

Molting

Baby snakes begin eating right away. Their bodies grow quickly, but their skin does not grow. Soon, their skin becomes too tight. Snakes molt their skin so that they can grow bigger. Young snakes molt many times before they are adults.

This young rattlesnake is molting.

This rattlesnake is an adult. It can mate and have babies of its own.

A lizard's life cycle

Like snakes, lizards are reptiles. Lizards have two pairs of legs, long bodies, and tails. Komodo dragons are big lizards. They can grow to be three feet (0.9 m) long! A Komodo dragon's life cycle is similar to the life cycles of many other kinds of lizards.

Komodo dragons are endangered animals. There are only a few thousand Komodo dragons left on Earth.

The life cycle of a Komodo dragon

A Komodo dragon's life cycle begins inside an egg. A Komodo dragon mother lays her eggs in a nest in the sand. After eight months, a hatchling hatches from each egg. The hatchling eats small lizards and birds. It grows and changes.

After about a year, the Komodo dragon is a juvenile. A juvenile Komodo dragon hunts bigger animals. It hunts wild pigs, monkeys, and deer. A Komodo dragon becomes an adult when it is six years old. As an adult, the Komodo dragon can mate and make its own babies.

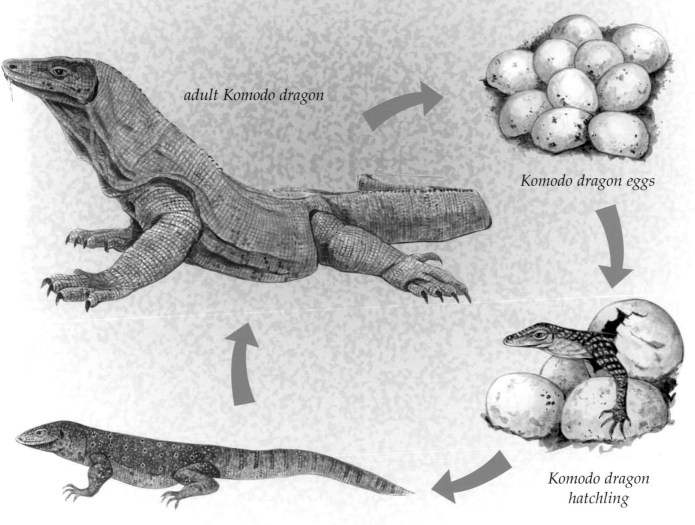

adult Komodo dragon

Komodo dragon eggs

Komodo dragon hatchling

juvenile Komodo dragon

Fish life cycles

A baby salmon has just hatched from its egg.

Most **fish** lay eggs. Some fish lay thousands of eggs. Others lay just a few eggs. Some fish hide their eggs in their mouths or in pouches on their bodies. The jawfish above is carrying its eggs in its mouth. Fish hide their eggs to protect them from **predators**. After baby fish hatch, they must protect themselves and find their own food.

A sea horse's life cycle

Sea horses are fish. Unlike other fish, mother sea horses do not lay their eggs. Instead, they pass their eggs to father sea horses. Male sea horses have pouches on the front of their bodies. The pouches hold the eggs. The embryos grow and hatch inside the pouches.

Leaving the pouch

Baby sea horses are called **fry**. When the fry are big enough to find food on their own, they swim out of the pouches. After a few weeks, young sea horses are juveniles. It takes up to one year for a juvenile to become an adult sea horse.

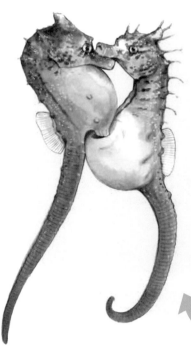

Adult sea horses can make babies. A female sea horse passes her eggs into the father sea horse's pouch. The father sea horse will carry the eggs in his pouch for two to four weeks.

Sea horse embryos grow inside eggs.

The fry hatch and leave their father's pouch. The fry find their own food.

Juvenile sea horses are not yet fully grown.

From egg to frog

Frogs are **amphibians**. Amphibians are animals that begin their lives in water, but as adults, they live mainly on land. Mother frogs lay their eggs in water. The babies that hatch from the eggs are called **tadpoles**. Tadpoles live in water.

Changing bodies

Most young animals look like their parents, but tadpoles do not look anything like adult frogs! Their bodies change completely before they become adults. This total change is called **complete metamorphosis**. When tadpoles are finished changing, they are frogs that can live on land.

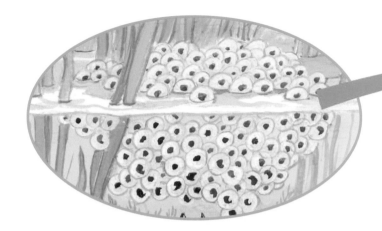

*Frog eggs are called **spawn**. Spawn look like blobs of jelly. They float on shallow water in ponds and lakes.*

A frog is fully grown. It can mate with another frog and make babies of its own.

A tadpole hatches from each egg. A newly hatched tadpole lives in water. It has a tail that helps it swim. The tadpole does not have legs. Like a fish, it has body parts called **gills** for breathing under water.

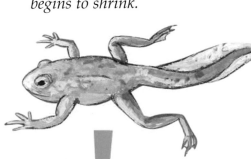

Before long, the tadpole's body begins to change. The tadpole grows back legs.

As the tadpole continues to change, it grows front legs, as well. The tadpole's body gets bigger, and its tail begins to shrink.

The tadpole keeps growing until it is almost an adult. Its tail is nearly gone. It has lungs inside its body for breathing air. The tadpole can now live on land.

Insect changes

Insects are a large group of animals. Many insects go through complete metamorphosis during their life cycles. Ladybugs are beetles. Ladybugs go through complete metamorphosis. The four stages of a ladybug's life cycle are egg, **larva**, **pupa**, and adult.

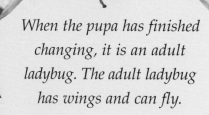

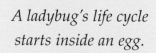

A ladybug's life cycle starts inside an egg.

When the pupa has finished changing, it is an adult ladybug. The adult ladybug has wings and can fly.

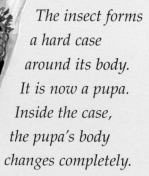

The insect forms a hard case around its body. It is now a pupa. Inside the case, the pupa's body changes completely.

A larva hatches from each egg. Each larva molts as it grows.

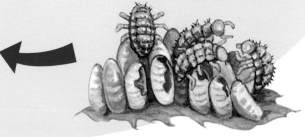

A grasshopper's life cycle

Some insects do not go through complete metamorphosis. Their life cycles have three stages instead of four. The insects begin their lives inside eggs, grow into **nymphs**, and then become adults. This set of changes is called **incomplete metamorphosis**. Grasshoppers are insects that go through incomplete metamorphosis.

A mother grasshopper lays her eggs in soil. She covers the eggs with white liquid from her body. The soil and the liquid keep the eggs warm.

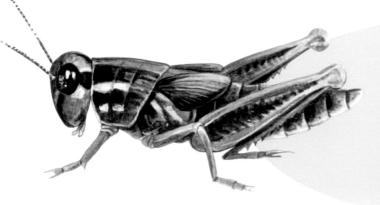

The grasshoppers that hatch from the eggs are called nymphs. Nymphs do not yet have all their adult body parts. Their wings are very small. Nymphs molt several times. Each time they molt, their wings grow larger.

The bodies of adult grasshoppers are fully grown. Adult grasshoppers have large wings and can fly. They can also make babies.

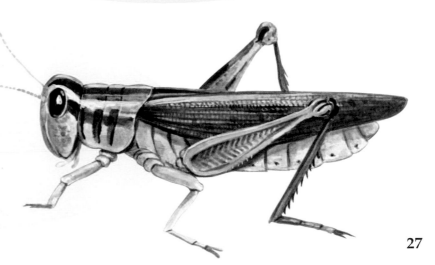

27

Spider changes

Spiders are not insects. Insects have six legs, but spiders have eight legs. A spider begins its life cycle inside an egg. A mother spider lays many eggs and then wraps them in an **egg sac**. She spins the egg sac out of silk. The spider mother makes the silk inside her body. There may be thousands of eggs in one egg sac!

Spiderlings, or baby spiders, hatch from their eggs inside the egg sac. Soon after they hatch, the spiderlings leave the egg sac.

Most spiderlings must take care of themselves after hatching. A few kinds of spider mothers feed and protect their spiderlings, however.

As a spiderling grows, its body becomes too big for its skin. It molts several times. After each molt, a new skin hardens over its body.

A fully grown spider is an adult. The bodies of most female adult spiders are larger than the bodies of male adult spiders.

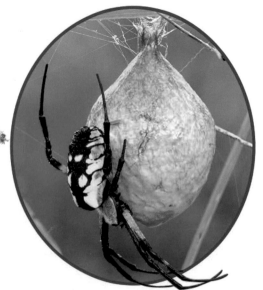

Wee worms

Adult earthworms have both male body parts and female body parts. Having both male and female parts means that all adult earthworms can lay eggs.

Before an earthworm can lay eggs, it must mate with another worm. After mating, both worms lay eggs. Earthworms lay eggs in **cocoons**, or protective cases.

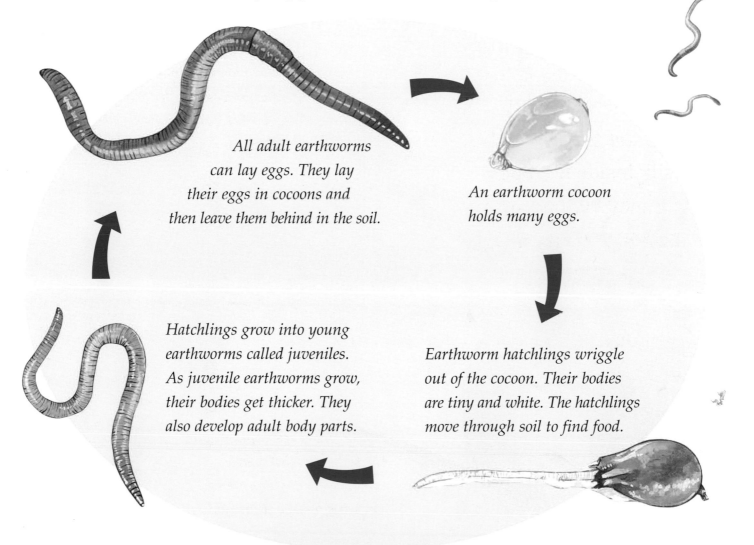

All adult earthworms can lay eggs. They lay their eggs in cocoons and then leave them behind in the soil.

An earthworm cocoon holds many eggs.

Hatchlings grow into young earthworms called juveniles. As juvenile earthworms grow, their bodies get thicker. They also develop adult body parts.

Earthworm hatchlings wriggle out of the cocoon. Their bodies are tiny and white. The hatchlings move through soil to find food.

More changes

An adult animal is in the last stage of its life cycle. For some animals, the adult stage lasts only a few days. For other animals, the adult stage lasts many years. Adult animals that live for many years may go through more changes as they get older. They may lose their teeth or may not be able to move as quickly as they did when they were younger. An animal dies when its body stops working. The length of time an animal is expected to live is called its **life span**.

Predators hunt other animals for food. This leopard has killed an impala. Many animals do not live their full life spans because they are killed or die from diseases.

Life cycle quiz

How much do you remember about the life cycles of animals? Take this quiz to find out!

1. How long do kits live with mother raccoons?
2. Where does a Komodo dragon mother lay her eggs?
3. How long do monk seals nurse?
4. Why do humpback whales migrate?
5. Where does a koala joey live after it is born?
6. Name three ways that tadpoles change as they grow.
7. How are spider eggs protected?
8. What is the third stage in a ladybug's life cycle?
9. Does a female sea horse carry her eggs?
10. What happens to snakes as they grow?

Answers

1. Raccoon kits live with their mothers for about a year.
2. A Komodo dragon mother lays her eggs in a nest in the sand.
3. Monk seals nurse for six weeks.
4. Humpbacks migrate to have their calves in warm oceans. Their calves cannot live in cold ocean waters.
5. A koala joey lives inside its mother's pouch after it is born.
6. Tadpoles lose their tails, grow legs, and develop lungs for breathing air.
7. Spider eggs are protected in egg sacs.
8. The third stage is the pupa.
9. No. A male sea horse carries the eggs.
10. Snakes molt as they grow.

Keep reading!

There is much more to learn about each of the life cycles shown in this book. There are books to read and websites to visit. Do not stop now! Keep reading! Check out this website:

- www.nationalgeographic.com/kids/creature_feature/archive

You may also want to check out these other "Bobbie Kalman" life cycle books:

- Insect Life Cycles
- Metamorphosis: Changing Bodies
- The Life Cycle of a Bat
- The Life Cycle of a Beetle
- The Life Cycle of a Bird
- The Life Cycle of a Butterfly
- The Life Cycle of a Flower
- The Life Cycle of a Frog
- The Life Cycle of a Honeybee
- The Life Cycle of a Koala
- The Life Cycle of a Lion
- The Life Cycle of a Mosquito
- The Life Cycle of a Polar Bear
- The Life Cycle of a Raccoon
- The Life Cycle of a Sea Horse
- The Life Cycle of a Sea Turtle
- The Life Cycle of a Shark
- The Life Cycle of a Snake
- The Life Cycle of a Spider
- The Life Cycle of a Tree
- The Life Cycle of a Whale
- The Life Cycle of a Wolf
- The Life Cycle of an Ant
- The Life Cycle of an Earthworm

Words to know

Note: Boldfaced words that are defined in the text may not appear on this page.

amphibian An animal that lives under water when it is young and lives on land when it is an adult; the word "amphibian" means "two lives"

bird An animal that has a beak, two wings, and feathers

complete metamorphosis The total change in an animal's body from one form to another

endangered Describes animals that are in danger of dying out in the wild

eucalyptus A type of tall tree that grows in Australia

fish An animal that lives under water and breathes using gills

insect An animal that has six legs and a hard outer covering on its body

larva The stage between egg and pupa in complete metamorphosis

mammal An animal that has fur or hair on its body and drinks its mother's milk when it is young

marine mammal A mammal that lives mainly in the ocean

marsupial A type of mammal; most female marsupials have pouches on their bodies

nymph The stage between egg and adult in incomplete metamorphosis

predator An animal that hunts and eats other animals

pupa The stage between larva and adult in complete metamorphosis

reptile An animal that has soft, scaly skin that molts as the animal grows

Index